Machines on the Farm

Siân Smith

Heinemann
LIBRARY

Chicago, Illinois

Edited by Dan Nunn and John-Paul Wilkins
Designed by Cynthia Akiyoshi
Picture research by Elizabeth Alexander
Production by Sophia Argyris
Originated by Capstone Global Library Ltd
Printed and bound in China by Leo Paper Products Ltd

17 16 15 14 13
10 9 8 7 6 5 4 3 2 1

Library of Congress Cataloging-in-Publication Data
Cataloging-in-Publication data is available at the Library
of Congress: loc.gov

ISBN 978-1-4329-7501-2 (hardback)
ISBN 978-1-4329-7506-7 (paperback)

Acknowledgments
We would like to thank the following for permission to
reproduce photographs: Alamy pp. 8 (© David R. Frazier
Photolibrary, Inc.), 14 (© AgStock Images, Inc.), 18, 23
milker (© Andrew Fox), 20 (© Joerg Boethling); Corbis
5 (© Juice Images), 15 (© Westend61); Getty Images
pp. 4 (Darrell Gulin/Stockbyte), 9 (Bloomberg), 16 (Alvis
Upitis/Stockbyte); Robert Harding p. title page (Emilio
Ferrer/age footstock); Shutterstock pp. 6 (© Orientaly),
7 (© V. J. Matthew), 10 (© Deyan Georgiev), 12, 23
harvest (© Jose Ignacio Soto), 13, 23 bale (© Rihardzz),
19 (© chinahbzyg), 21 (© spflaum), 23 grain (© IDAL),
23 rows (© Straight 8 Photography); SuperStock pp. 11,
23 pesticides (© imagebroker.net), 17 (© Tips Images),
22 (© The Irish Image Collection).

Design element photographs of car engine part (© fuyu
liu), gear cog (© Leremy), grain field (© haraldmuc),
and wheat field (© oriontrail) reproduced with
permission of Shutterstock.

Front cover photograph of reaping machine in a wheat
field reproduced with permission of Robert Harding
(Emilio Ferrer/age footstock). Back cover photograph of
tractor (© Orientaly) and baler (© Rihardzz) reproduced
with permission of Shutterstock.

We would like to thank Paul Charvill, Veronica Kitson,
Dee Reid, and Marla Conn for their invaluable help in
the preparation of this book.

Every effort has been made to contact copyright holders
of material reproduced in this book. Any omissions will
be rectified in subsequent printings if notice is given to
the publisher.

All the Internet addresses (URLs) given in this book were
valid at the time of going to press. However, due to the
dynamic nature of the Internet, some addresses may
have changed, or sites may have changed or ceased to
exist since publication. While the author and publisher
regret any inconvenience this may cause readers, no
responsibility for any such changes can be accepted by
either the author or the publisher.

Contents

OCT 0 7 2013

Some words are shown in bold, **like this**. You can find out what they mean by looking in the glossary.

Why Do We Have Machines On a Farm?

A farm is a place where animals are kept or plants are grown.

Farmers sell the plants and animals for people to eat.

There are many jobs that need to be done on farms.

Different machines make the jobs easier to do.

Which Farm Machines Are the Most Useful?

Tractors are very useful farm machines.

Their large back wheels help them to move in mud without getting stuck.

back wheel

plow

Farmers use tractors to pull many different farm machines.

A plow is used to dig up the ground before planting seeds.

Which Farm Machines Plant Seeds?

Planting machines pulled by tractors plant seeds or plants in the ground.

Seed drills plant seeds in **rows** in the soil.

seed drill

planter

Planters plant young plants in the ground.
Planting machines allow farmers to plant
many seeds or plants at a time.

How Do Machines Help Us to Grow Plants?

Farm machines can be used to water plants. Sometimes the water can be controlled by clocks called timers.

helicopter

Some machines spray **pesticides**, to kill insects that eat plants.

On some big farms, helicopters are used to spray pesticides.

Which Machines Help to Harvest Plants?

Combine harvesters help farmers to **harvest** or pick **grain** plants.

They cut the plants and collect the seeds. Then they take the seeds out of their cases and leave the straw behind.

bale

baler machine

Other machines take the straw, or hay, from cut grass and make it into **bales**.

They roll or crush it into round or square bales and tie it up.

Do All Harvesting Machines Look the Same?

Harvesting machines that pick and sort different types of plants can look very different.

Some large machines can be used to pick and sort tomatoes.

Grape picking machines have a large gap in the middle so that they can drive along **rows** of grape vines.

The machine shakes the grape vines and collects the grapes that fall down.

Some machines **harvest** vegetables that grow under the ground.

They pull the vegetables out or dig them up. The vegetables move along a belt, and the machine gets rid of the soil.

potatoes

belt

Some machines collect fruit that grows on trees.

Olive harvesters shake the trees and catch the fruit that falls off.

Which Farm Machine Milks Cows?

Farmers use a **milker** to milk cows.

The farmer puts a milker onto each cow's four teats.

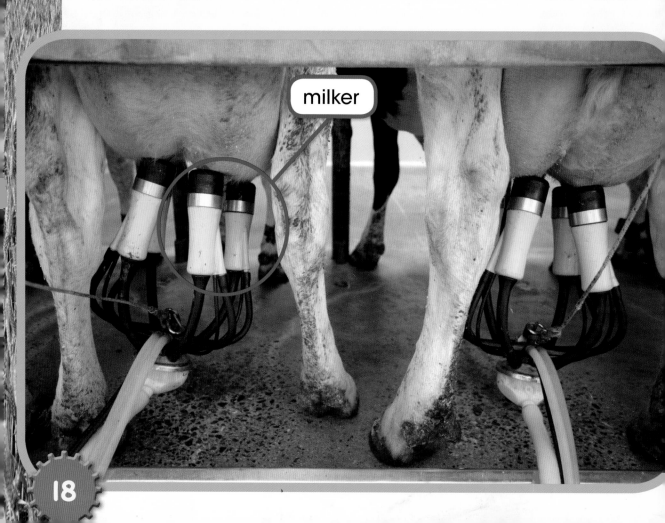

milker

When the machine starts, the milkers suck out milk. Pipes take the milk into large tanks to keep it cool.

When there is no more milk, the milkers drop off.

What Other Machines Are Used On a Farm?

Farmers use other machines to help with many different jobs.

Tree cutters and other machines are used to keep farms safe and neat.

Machines are used to sort or pack food items.

An egg sorter puts small, medium, and large eggs into cartons. The farmer can sell the different eggs at different prices.

What Does This Machine Do?

Can you guess what this machine does?
Find the answer on page 24.

Picture Glossary

bale hay or straw tied together in a bundle

grain seeds and cereals that come from grasses, including corn, wheat, and rice

harvest pick or collect

milker part of a machine used to milk cows. A milker sucks out milk from a cow's teats.

pesticide special liquid that is used on plants to kill insects

row line of things such as plants

23

Find Out More

Books

Coppendale, Jean. *Tractors and Farm Vehicles* (Mighty Machines). Irvine, Calif.: QEB, 2007.

Dickmann, Nancy. *Farm Machines* (World of Farming). Chicago: Heinemann Library, 2011.

Internet Sites

Facthound offers a safe, fun way to find Internet sites related to this book. All of the sites on Facthound have been researched by our staff.

Here's all you do:

Visit www.facthound.com

Type in this code: 9781432975012

Index

The farm machine on page 22 is spreading manure to help plants grow. Manure is made from animal waste.